PREHISTORIC SAFARI
GIANT DINOSAURS

Liz Miles

RiverStream

Hardcover edition first published in 2012 by Arcturus Publishing

Hardcover Library bound edition distributed by Black Rabbit Books
P. O. Box 3263
Mankato
Minnesota MN 56002

Published by arrangement with Arcturus Publishing

Library of Congress Cataloging-in-Publication Data

Miles, Liz.
 Giant dinosaurs / by Liz Miles.
    p. cm. – (Prehistoric safari)
 Includes index.
 ISBN 978-1-84858-568-3 (hardcover, library bound)
 1. Dinosaurs–Juvenile literature. I. Title.
 QE861.5.M5536 2013
 567.9–dc23

                      2011051443

Text: Liz Miles
Editor: Joe Harris
Picture researcher: Joe Harris
Design: Emma Randall
Cover design: Emma Randall

Picture credits:
De Agostini Picture Library: 7tr, 7cr, 9cr, 11br, 13br, 15tr, 19cr, 19br, 21tr, 23cr, 25br,
27tr, 27cr, 27br. Highlights for Children, Inc.: 7br, 15cr, 19tr. iStockphoto: 11tr, 11cr. Miles
Kelly Publishing Ltd: 13cr, 23tr, 23br. Natural History Museum, London: 13tr, 21cr, 21br.
pixel-shack.com: cover (main) 1, 5tr, 6–7, 8–9, 12–13, 14–15, 22–23, 24–25, 25tr, 28t.
Shutterstock: cover (top images) 2–3, 4–5, 5cr, tbr, 10–11, 16–17, 17tr, 17br, 18–19,
20–21, 26–27, 29 (all). Wikimedia: 9tr, 9br, 15br, 17cr, 25cr, 28b.

SL002122US

1 2 3 4 5 GPP 16 15 14 13
RiverStream Publishing—Globus Printing and Packaging, Minster, OH—082013—1037GPPSM13
Paperback version printed in the USA

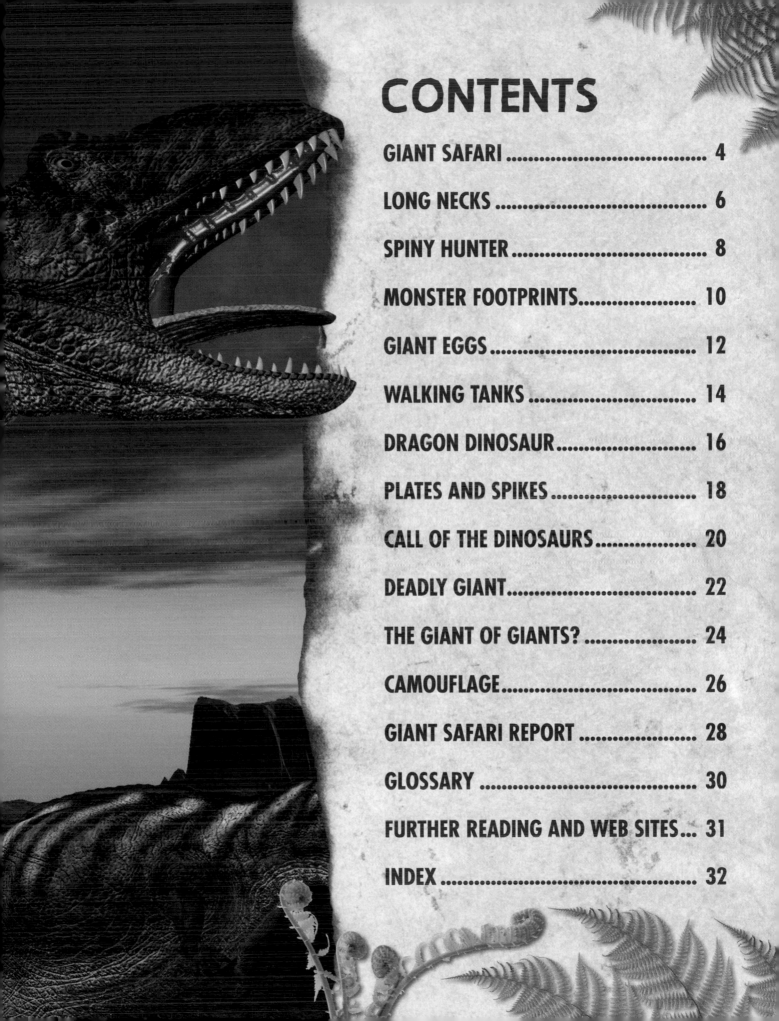

CONTENTS

GIANT SAFARI

Are you ready for a truly breathtaking adventure? You are about to parachute from a plane down to a secret island—an island full of huge prehistoric monsters. Your goal is to capture the biggest dinosaur of all on film. Your tracking skills, your sprinting ability, and your bravery are going to be essential.

As you fly over the island, a group of flying reptiles swoops dangerously close to your plane. They must be *Pteranodon*.

Soon you will be facing predators with teeth like swords and armored heavyweights like *Triceratops*—which could flatten you underfoot or impale you with its horns.

The pilot circles low, looking for a safe landing site for your parachute jump. You stare from the window, amazed that the island is home to creatures that are meant to have died out 65 million years ago.

SAFARI ESSENTIALS

Gingko leaves Some of the biggest dinosaurs are plant-eaters, so tasty leaves from this tree might prove a useful distraction. Gingkos are called "living fossils," as similar plants existed up to 270 million years ago.

Camera Your friends are unlikely to believe what you see on safari—so you will need lots of photos as proof. A good zoom lens means you won't have to get too close.

dinoPad All the dinosaur facts you need to know have been downloaded onto your electronic reader.

LONG NECKS

The parachute drop is over in seconds. The breeze carries you down onto a wet, sandy beach, right next to a herd of gigantic *Brachiosaurus*. They call to each other—do they see you as a threat? You back away from their powerful tails and quickly gather up the parachute. Then you follow the giants as they amble along the beach, into a forested area.

As high as a ten-story building, a *Brachiosaurus* can stretch its long neck to graze on the topmost leaves of conifer trees. It leaves footprints 40 in (1 m) long.

Its chisel-like teeth are good for cutting but not chewing. To help digest tough leaves, it swallows stones that grind the greens in its giant-sized stomach.

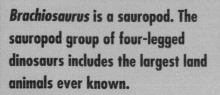

Brachiosaurus is a sauropod. The sauropod group of four-legged dinosaurs includes the largest land animals ever known.

Meaning of name: Arm lizard
Height: 50 ft (15 m)
Length: 100 ft (30 m)
Family: Brachiosauridae
Period: Late Jurassic
Weight: 88 tons (80,000 kg)
Found in: Algeria, Portugal, Tanzania, USA
Diet: Plants

GRAZERS

Many of the biggest dinosaurs are herbivores (plant-eaters).

▼ *Alamosaurus*
In spite of its size, the powerful back legs of the *Alamosaurus* are strong enough to take its full weight when stretching to reach the topmost branches of trees.

▶ **Iguanodon**
The plant-eating *Iguanodon* has tough teeth in its beaklike mouth for grinding up plants.

◀ **Prehistoric plants**
Flowering plants did not become common until the Cretaceous period. Before that, sauropods had to feed on tough-leaved evergreens, such as conifers and cycads.

SPINY HUNTER

You slip cautiously through the sharp-leaved plants to a sunlit swamp, where you come across a huge predator. The creature—a *Spinosaurus*— is peering into a pool of water. Suddenly it snatches up a fish. You see sharp teeth and catch the stench of its foul breath. Then it turns and looks straight at you. Time to make a quick escape!

Unlike other meat-eating dinosaurs, spinosaurids have a long, narrow snout and small, sharp teeth—useful for snapping up slippery fish.

Spinosaurids eat mainly carrion and fish. The big claws on their thumbs are used for defense and to grasp fish.

The "sail" of skin and bone on the *Spinosaurus'* back might be used like a solar panel to help heat up its body and a car radiator to cool it down, or for display.

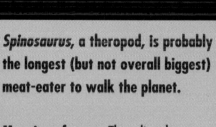

Spinosaurus, a theropod, is probably the longest (but not overall biggest) meat-eater to walk the planet.

Meaning of name: Thorn lizard
Height: 17 ft (5 m)
Length: 52 ft (16 m)
Family: Spinosauridae
Period: Late Cretaceous
Weight: 4 tons (3,600 kg)
Found in: Egypt, Morocco
Diet: Meat

SAILS AND FINS

▶ *Spinosaurus*
The *Spinosaurus'* "sail" contains spines that stand up from the backbone, up to 6.5 ft (2 m) high.

▼ *Acrocanthosaurus* is a killer with a small fin down its back. This is thicker than *Spinosaur*'s sail and might be used for fat storage or signalling.

▼ *Dimetrodon* The 10 ft- (3 m-) high *Dimetrodon* is the most aggressive predator of the Permian period. It has an impressive sail that must terrify its prey.

MONSTER FOOTPRINTS

You run until you are out of breath, and clear of the trees. There you find a set of prints, which you start to follow. Before long, you discover the source of the trail—a herd of *Diplodocus*. You used to think of these as gentle giants, but now realize their tails are powerful weapons. Something flashes before your eyes! You crouch to avoid another crack of the "whip."

Diplodocus' pencil-sharp teeth, downturned head, and long neck are used to feed on a wide area of low-growing plants. It grazes like a cow.

There are nostrils on the top of its head—useful to sniff the air for likely predators as it grazes.

The head is small compared to the body, with room for just a tiny brain. It is not very intelligent.

Diplodocus is one of the most famous dinosaurs and travels in grazing herds.

Meaning of name: Double beam
Height: 16 ft (5 m)
Length: 90 ft (27 m)
Family: Diplodocidea
Period: Late Jurassic
Weight: 12 tons (11,000 kg)
Found in: United States
Diet: Plants

FEET AND FOOTPRINTS
Fossil footprints show how dinosaurs walked.

◄ *Diplodocus* leaves huge back footprints and smaller front footprints. It walks on thick pads and three toes, built to take the weight of its massive body. The front feet have sharp thumb claws. It walks slowly.

► *Tyrannosaurus* and other meat-eaters leave large, birdlike footprints. They move on two legs, and can run fast. Three of the four toes on each foot touch the ground.

▼ *Triceratops* leave smaller prints than long-necked sauropods, but their depth shows the heavy weight of their bodies. They are slow, plodding walkers.

GIANT EGGS

While crouching, you spot something that looks like a white football. A closer look at the "ball," and you realize it's a huge egg. Then you see another, and another. The last is warm, recently laid. A few more steps and there's the spectacular egg-layer—an *Apatosaurus*, even sturdier looking than a *Diplodocus*. It wanders off, leaving the eggs to hatch alone.

Apatosaurus does not take care of its eggs or its newly hatched young. The eggs are an easy meal for predators.

Apatosaurus lays its eggs as it walks, each egg dropping about 8 ft (2.5 m) onto the ground without breaking.

Apatosaurus eggs are up to 1 ft (30 cm) in diameter.

Apatosaurus (once known as a *Brontosaurus*) is a massive sauropod, but harmless—unless it steps on you.

Meaning of name: Deceptive lizard
Height: 13 ft (4 m)
Length: 70 ft (21 m)
Family: Diplodocidea
Period: Late Jurassic
Weight: 33 tons (30,000 kg)
Found in: United States
Diet: Plants

EGGS AND NESTS

▶ Eggs are a perfect meal for a beaky dinosaur like *Gallimimus*. Its long, toothless jaws can easily crack the shell of a small dinosaur egg.

▼ Most dinosaurs lay their eggs in nests (a mound of soil or mud), like *Maiasaura* (which means "good-mother lizard"). *Maiasaura* may look after their young for years and travel with them in herds.

▼ The biggest dinosaur egg fossils ever found are ellipsoid in shape and 16 in (41 cm) long.

WALKING TANKS

You soon come across four awesome, horned monsters—the tanklike *Triceratops*! These creatures seem to be on edge, so you are relieved to remember they are herbivores. You witness a head-to-head combat between two males. Horns crack and crash. The whole forest shakes as another joins in. It's time to beat a hasty retreat, before you are trampled...

The three sharp horns are used to battle with other males as they fight over mates. They are also useful for fighting off predators. By stabbing the underbellies of dinosaurs like *Tyrannosaurus* they can escape.

The frill protects the vulnerable neck from a deadly bite, tearing claw, or jabbing horn.

Triceratops' teeth are like shears, perfect for chomping through low-growing plants.

Triceratops is a fearsome, three-horned plant-eater.

Meaning of name: Three-horned face
Height: 10 ft (3 m)
Length: 30 ft (9 m)
Family: Ceratopidae
Period: Late Cretaceous
Weight: 6 tons (5,400 kg)
Found in: United States
Diet: Plants

FRILLED FACES

▼ *Chasmosaurus* has a huge, rectangular neck frill. Instead of solid bone, which would have been too heavy, it is made up of bone struts, with skin stretched across.

◄ *Styracosaurus* can form a wall of defense with their 2-ft- (60-cm-) long horns and frills, by gathering in herds. The younger, more vulnerable, *Styracosaurus* are protected by staying near the middle.

▶ *Centrosaurus* has a frill that is too thin for defense. Instead, it may have been for show, to scare off predators, or to attract mates. This skull shows the holes in the frill, which make it lighter.

DRAGON DINOSAUR

You follow a rustling in the trees—and almost run into the mouth of a dragonlike *Ceratosaurus*! You clamber up a conifer tree, but only just in time. You cling tight—one slip and you will be minced by those bladelike teeth. Suddenly the predator swings its head away, spots some easier prey, and strides away.

The horns and jagged crest down the back of the *Ceratosaurus* are for show.

This giant can run fast to catch its prey, and has jaws large enough to kill at a single bite.

Ceratosaurus is one of the most common predators in late-Jurassic times, so where there is one, there are likely to be more.

IN THE JAWS OF THE GIANTS

Ceratosaurus is a member of the same family as *Allosaurus* and was at the top of the food chain where it lived.

Meaning of name: Horned lizard
Height: 13 ft (4 m)
Length: 20 ft (6 m)
Family: Ceratosauridae
Period: Late Jurassic
Weight: 1.4 tons (1,300 kg)
Found in: United States
Diet: Meat

The curved claws are well designed for giving deadly blows and for ripping the flesh from a carcass.

▶ Giant meat-eating theropods like *Tyrannosaurus rex* and *Ceratosaurus* have some of the biggest teeth—up to 9 in (23 cm) in length. They are pointed and sharp for tearing flesh and crushing bones.

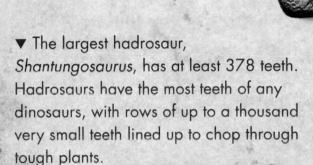

▼ The largest hadrosaur, *Shantungosaurus*, has at least 378 teeth. Hadrosaurs have the most teeth of any dinosaurs, with rows of up to a thousand very small teeth lined up to chop through tough plants.

▶ Giant sauropods like *Apatosaurus* have small heads and teeth less than 1.6 in (4 cm) long. Their peglike teeth are only useful for biting off leaves to eat.

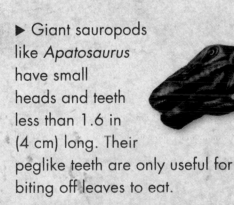

PLATES AND SPIKES

Taking care not to be spotted, you observe the killer's new prey—a lone *Stegosaurus*. It thrashes its spiked tail and raises its plated back to warn off the predator. Surprisingly, the *Ceratosaurus* wanders off, leaving the *Stegosaurus* to warm its kite-shaped plates in the evening sun. You pitch your tent and eat your one hot meal of the day.

The plates are probably just for show, or to help regulate the dinosaur's body temperature.

The two rows of back plates are too weak to protect the dinosaur from an attack. No one knows for sure what their purpose is.

Stegosaurus has the jaws and teeth to graze and grind. Its cheeks can store food for chewing later.

Stegosaurus is the largest member of the plant-eating family of stegosaurs.

Meaning of name: Roof lizard
Height: 9 ft (2.8 m)
Length: 30 ft (9 m)
Family: Stegosauridae
Period: Late Jurassic
Weight: 3 tons (2,700 kg)
Found in: United States
Diet: Plants

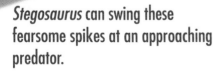

Stegosaurus can swing these fearsome spikes at an approaching predator.

BODY ARMOR

▼ *Saltasaurus* relies on real armor. Its back is covered in small, hornlike bumps, with strong, bony discs under the skin's surface.

▼ *Nodosaurus* is the height of an adult human. Like a tortoise, it can crouch under its bony plates and wait for any predator to tire of trying to break through.

▼ *Wuerhosaurus* has a spiked tail like the *Stegosaurus*, and two rows of back plates too. Stegosaur tails are called "thagomizers." Some bear up to ten deadly spikes.

CALL OF THE DINOSAURS

You are woken by a hornlike alarm. Outside your tent you find a brightly colored beast with a curious crest—a *Parasaurolophus*. It blasts its "horn" again, then a smaller creature comes thundering through the trees. It's a female, attracted to the sound of its mate. However, another creature has also heard the call of the duck-billed dinosaur. These creatures are its favorite prey.

Parasaurolophus is called a duck-billed dinosaur because its beaklike snout is similar to a modern duck's bill.

Meaning of name: Ridged lizard
Height: 9 ft (2.8 m)
Length: 33 ft (10 m)
Family: Hadrosauridae
Period: Late Cretaceous
Weight: 3 tons (2,700 kg)
Found in: Canada, United States
Diet: Plants

The swept back, curved crest, and tail form a streamlined shape that can slip between the undergrowth without being seen.

Tubes in the crest make the hadrosaur's call louder.

The larger crest means that other *Parasaurolophus* recognize it as a male.

A snort from this creature sounds like a blast from a horn or a trombone.

▼ ***Corythosaurus*** Like the other plant-eating hadrosaurs, *Corythosaurus* has a cutting beak and a mouth crammed with grinding teeth.

▼ ***Edmontosaurus*** This hadrosaur may inflate its nose to show off. Some scientists think it blows up the loose skin around its nose in the same way a toad blows up a pouch under its chin.

▼ ***Lambeosaurus*** Like other hadrosaurs, *Lambeosaurus* is a herd dweller. Group living provides safety in numbers, and colorful crests are a useful way of identifying family members.

DEADLY GIANT

Trapped between a *Giganotosaurus* and its prey, you stand frozen with fear. The hungry killer snarls from 36 feet (11 m) above. You nervously admire its clawed fingers, powerful jaw, vicious teeth, and intelligent eyes. It moves slowly, staring at you and the hadrosaurs. It lurches forward, you scream… and then you are saved by a shadow.

Giganotosaurus are the largest known carnivorous dinosaurs.

Unlike *Tyrannosaurus rex*, whose teeth are shaped for crushing and tearing flesh and bone, *Giganotosaurus* has teeth that are flatter and more daggerlike, which work like meat-slicers.

Giganotosaurus is thought to be the largest theropod, but not the biggest dinosaur.

Meaning of name: Giant southern lizard
Height: 10 ft (3 m)
Length: 43 ft (13 m)
Family: Allosauridae
Period: Mid Cretaceous
Weight: 6 tons (5,400 kg)
Found in: Argentina
Diet: Meat

Muscular hind legs and a large tail for balance means *Giganotosaurus* can run fast, in spite of its weight.

BIG AND BRAINY?

A bigger brain in relation to the body of a dinosaur often suggests greater intelligence.

▼ *Tyrannosaurus rex* Although *T. rex* (shown here) has a slightly smaller body than the *Giganotosaurus*, its brain is bigger. Both need large brains as hunting requires intelligence, good eyesight, and speed.

▶ *Troodon* has a big brain and big eyes, and is often described as the brightest of dinosaurs.

▼ *Stegosaurus* This huge creature's brain is the size of a lemon. Some scientists believe it may have another brain elsewhere in its body.

THE GIANT OF GIANTS?

The sky turns black as the dinosaur you've been seeking looms, casting a mountain-sized shadow. You blink, look up, and see the magnificent form of what is probably the biggest dinosaur to have lived—*Argentinosaurus*. The *Giganotosaurus* almost drools at the sight of such a vast meal. Suddenly you are aware of being in the middle of what could be the most violent dinosaur battle ever, so you run for your life.

Colossal sauropods like *Argentinosaurus* need lots of food as they grow into adults. An adolescent probably gains as much as 100 pounds (45 kg) of weight each day.

Argentinosaurus, a sauropod, may be the tallest and heaviest land animal ever to have existed.

Meaning of name: Argentina lizard
Height: 70 ft (21 m)
Length: 120 ft (36 m)
Family: Antarctosauridae
Period: Late Cretaceous
Weight: 121 tons (110,000 kg)
Found in: Argentina
Diet: Plants

Argentinosaurus weighs more than 15 fully-grown elephants put together.

WEIGHING UP THE EVIDENCE

▶ *Argentinosaurus* Little has been found of this dinosaur, but scientists have estimated its size by measuring vertebrae (back bones). Many are 5 ft (1.5 m) tall by 5 ft (1.5 m) wide. That's as tall as an adult human!

▼ *Amphicoelias* will always be a contender for the biggest dinosaur, but the only fossil ever found has been lost—just a drawing exists (see below).

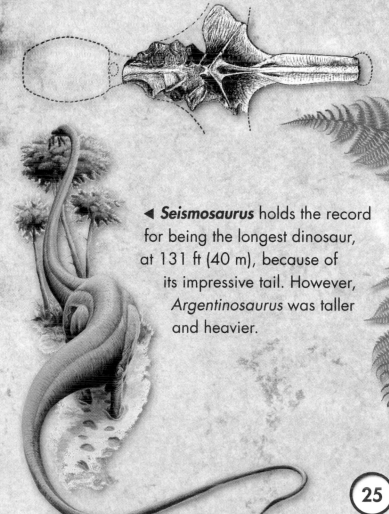

◀ *Seismosaurus* holds the record for being the longest dinosaur, at 131 ft (40 m), because of its impressive tail. However, *Argentinosaurus* was taller and heavier.

CAMOUFLAGE

The sun is setting. It's time to head for the shore, where a boat is due to pick you up and take you home. You wade through the marshes and stop briefly to gaze at familiar markings on unfamiliar creatures. Just as giraffes have camouflage, so do these giant sauropods! You know why they need to hide—you've met some of the terrifying predators they fear.

The *Dicraeosaurus* has an unusually short neck and relatively large head for a sauropod.

As on a giraffe, patches or spots help hide the dinosaur when it is among the shadows of trees.

Dicraeosaurus browse in areas with other plant-eaters, *Giraffatitan* and *Kentrosaurus*. Because each of these is a different height, they eat plants at different levels, so there's no fighting over the juiciest leaves.

Dicraeosaurus is in the same family as *Diplodocus* and has a whiplike tail that is used as a weapon.

Meaning of name: Two forked lizard
Height: 12 ft (3.7 m)
Length: 66 ft (20 m)
Family: Diplodocidae
Period: Late Jurassic
Weight: 6 tons (5,400 kg)
Found in: Tanzania
Diet: Plants

Like all dinosaurs, *Dicraeosaurus* could not swim, but probably waded into rivers for a drink, to cool down, or to escape a passing predator.

COLORFUL DINOSAURS

How do we know about dinosaurs' skin colors and patterns?

▼ **Evidence** Mummified skin tissue from a 67 million-year-old hadrosaur shows that the dinosaur had skin scales of different sizes, suggesting stripes or other patterns. But until we know for sure, artists must use their imagination.

▼ **Camouflage** An armored dinosaur like *Polacanthus* may have had markings that meant they could crouch and hide from predators among the undergrowth.

▶ **Feathers** Fossil evidence shows that many dinosaurs, such as this *Syntarsus*, had feathers for insulation or display.

GIANT SAFARI REPORT

On your way home, you look at the photographs you have taken on your safari. The picture that still makes you shudder is your snap of the *Giganotosaurus*. What could be more terrifying than a giant killer with teeth like sharp knives? And you were within inches of it!

Paleontologists are still trying to work out which of the giants is the size record-holder. New fossils and discoveries are being made all the time, which means a final decision is impossible. Some scientists believe that *Argentinosaurus* is the largest dinosaur ever to have lived. Others argue that *Amphicoelias* or *Bruhathkayosaurus* could have been even bigger (see below). In the future, fossils of even larger monsters may be discovered!

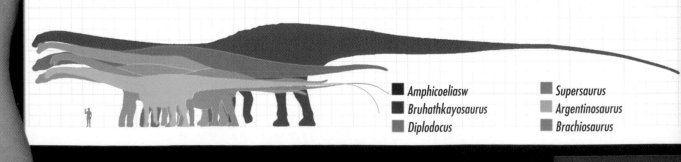

- Amphicoeliasw
- Bruhathkayosaurus
- Diplodocus
- Supersaurus
- Argentinosaurus
- Brachiosaurus

The incredible inhabitants of your safari location originally lived at two different times during the prehistoric era.

JURASSIC 200 million to 150 million years ago

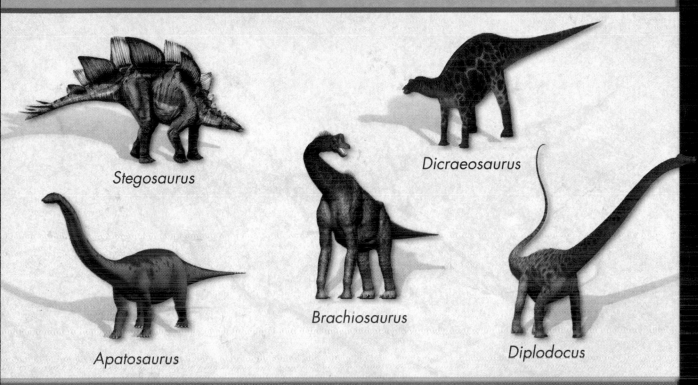

Stegosaurus

Dicraeosaurus

Apatosaurus

Brachiosaurus

Diplodocus

CRETACEOUS 150 million to 65 million years ago

Giganotosaurus

Ceratosaurus

Parasaurolophus

Spinosaurus

Triceratops

Argentinosaurus

GLOSSARY

camouflage Colorings or markings that make something blend into its setting so that it cannot be seen so easily.

carcass The body of a dead creature.

carrion Flesh from a creature that has died, and a source of food for some animals, such as hyenas.

conifer trees Trees that have needle-shaped leaves and bear cones; examples today are fir and pine trees.

Cretaceous A prehistoric period in which mammals and giant dinosaurs such as *Tyrannosaurus rex* lived. This period ended with the mass extinction of the dinosaurs 65 million years ago.

cycad A type of palm tree that was common in the Jurassic age.

duck-billed dinosaurs Dinosaurs with jaws that are shaped like a duck's bill (beak); also called hadrosaurids.

ellipsoid Oval in shape.

evergreens Plants that have green leaves all year round.

food chain A group of living things that are linked by what eats what; an example of a food chain is a fox eating a rat, and the rat eating an insect, and the insect eating a plant.

fossils Prehistoric remains such as bones or traces such as footprints that have become preserved in rock.

frill A bony area around the neck of a dinosaur.

grazing Feeding on low-growing plants, just as cows feed on grass.

hadrosaurs Plant-eating dinosaurs, also known as duck-billed dinosaurs because of their beaklike mouths.

insulation A way of keeping warm; for example, feathers insulate birds by keeping the warmth in and the cold out.

Jurassic A prehistoric period between 200 and 150 million years ago, during which a huge number of dinosaurs lived.

living fossil A plant or creature that lives today but also lived in prehistoric times in a similar form.

mammals Animals that give birth to live young and feed their young milk. They are warm-blooded.

mummified Preserved in a way that slows down the process of decay. The Egyptians famously mummified their pharaohs, but mummification also happens in nature.

paleontologist A person who studies prehistoric times and evidence such as fossils and rocks.

plates Bony sections on the outer body of a dinosaur that form a kind of armor, or stand up from the spine as on a *Stegosaurus*.

predator An animal that hunts other animals to kill and eat.

prey An animal that is hunted by other animals for food.

reptiles Animals that have scales and cold blood and lay eggs.

sauropod A giant, four-legged, plant-eating dinosaur with a small head but a long neck and tail.

spinosaurids Large two-legged, meat-eating dinosaurs that lived in the Cretaceous period.

streamline The smooth shape of a body or object that helps it move more easily through, for example, woods, water, or the air.

theropods Two-footed, mainly meat-eating dinosaurs such as *Tyrannosaurus rex* and *Giganotosaurus*.

FURTHER READING

Amazing Giant Dinosaurs (DK Children, 2012)

Dinosaur Encyclopedia by Caroline Bingham (Dorling Kindersley, 2009)

Giganotosaurus: The Giant Southern Lizard by Rob Shone (PowerKids Press, 2008)

National Geographic Kids Ultimate Dinopedia: The Most Complete Dinosaur Reference Ever by Don Lessum (National Geographic, 2010)

Princeton Field Guide to Dinosaurs by Gregory S. Paul (Princeton University Press, 2010)

Triceratops Vs Stegosaurus: When Horns and Plates Collide (Dinosaur Wars) by Michael O'Hearn (Raintree, 2011)

WEB SITES

www.amnh.org/exhibitions/fightingdinos/—Information about the American Museum of Natural History's "Fighting Dinosaurs"

http://dsc.discovery.com Discovery Dinosaur Central—search the DinoViewer for size comparisons and how dinosaurs moved

http://ngm.nationalgeographic.com National Geographic—search for the Bizarre Dinosaur section for a closer look at strange dinosaurs

www.nhm.ac.uk/kids-only/dinosaurs/index.html London's Natural History Museum—includes a dinosaur directory and quiz

http://www.jurassicpark.com/site/ Jurassic Park—explore a fictional world of dinosaurs

INDEX

PREHISTORIC SAFARI

KILLER DINOSAURS

Liz Miles

RiverStream

Hardcover edition first published in 2012 by Arcturus Publishing

Hardcover Library bound edition distributed by Black Rabbit Books
P. O. Box 3263
Mankato
Minnesota MN 56002

Published by arrangement with Arcturus Publishing

Library of Congress Cataloging-in-Publication Data

Miles, Liz.
 Killer dinosaurs / by Liz Miles.
    p. cm. – (Prehistoric safari)
 Includes index.
 ISBN 978 1 84858-569-0 (hardcover, library bound)
 1. Dinosaurs–Juvenile literature. I. Title.
 QE861.5.M5537 2013
 567.9–dc23

                    2011051449

Text: Liz Miles
Editor: Joe Harris
Picture researcher: Joe Harris
Design: Emma Randall
Cover design: Emma Randall

Picture credits:
De Agostini Picture Library: 7tr, 7br, 13br, 15cr, 9tr, 19cr, 19br, 29tr, 29br. Highlights
for Children, Inc: 15tr. Miles Kelly Publishing Ltd: 11cr, 11br, 15br, 17br, 21tr. National
Geographic: 2–3, 24–25, 25tr, 25cr. Natural History Museum, London: 7cr, 13tr, 21cr.
pixel-shack.com: cover (main), 1, 5br, 8–9, 10–11, 11tr, 12–13, 14–15, 16–17, 17cr,
18–19, 20–21, 22–23, 23tr, 26–27, 28t, 29tc. Shutterstock: cover (all images top row),
4–5, 5tr, 5cr, 6–7, 9cr, 9br, 17tr, 23br, 27tr, 27cr, 27br, 29 (all except tc, tr, br).
Wikimedia: 13cr, 21br, 23cr, 25br.

SL002123US

1 2 3 4 5 GPP 16 15 14 13
RiverStream Publishing—Globus Printing and Packaging, Minster, OH—082013—1037GPPSM13
Paperback version printed in the USA

CONTENTS

KILLER SAFARI

Are you ready for the adventure of a lifetime? You're about to set off on a journey across a mysterious island where killer dinosaurs live. Your mission is to film the most terrifying monsters of the prehistoric past. You will come face-to-face with hungry meat-eaters. This safari is going to be incredibly risky!

Before you set out, you check that you have all your supplies. To cope with the tricky island terrain—and to make quick escapes from deadly dinosaurs—you have brought an ATV (all terrain vehicle).

Soon you will be meeting killer dinosaurs like *Tyrannosaurus rex*—its head is nearly as long as you are tall. Beware those giant teeth. They could crush you like a bug!

SAFARI ESSENTIALS

Bones You are unlikely to need bones for bait—hungry dinosaurs will smell you out. However, a tasty bone might distract a charging killer long enough for you to escape.

Video camera As well as still shots of dinosaurs, video recordings are essential for capturing them in battle.

Your boat anchors offshore. You nervously drive your ATV down a ramp, through shallow waters, and across a rocky shore. You gasp at the sight of howling *Apatosaurus* as you speed over a grassy hill.

dinoPad All the dinosaur facts you need have been downloaded onto your electronic reader. You'll know which dinosaurs to fear the most.

SMALL BUT DEADLY

Just five minutes into your safari, you are reminded that killers come in all sizes. A herd of *Compsognathus* runs past, their bodies little bigger than chickens. You see one snap up a lizard, then run off, chewing noisily. You have barely set up your camera when something bigger suddenly looms into shot…

It stretches its flexible, long neck to catch prey between its small, sharp teeth.

The long tail helps it keep its balance as it runs.

The grasping fingers are useful for keeping a tight hold on a lizard or small mammal, ready for the first tasty bite.

Compsognathus is one of the smallest dinosaurs ever found.

Meaning of name: Pretty jaw
Height: 2 ft, 4 in (0.7 m)
Length: 4 ft, 7 in (1.4 m)
Family: Compsognathidae
Period: Late Cretaceous
Weight: 6.6 lb (3 kg)
Found in: France, Germany
Diet: Meat

The carnivorous (meat-eating) *Compsognathus* spends most of its time looking for small creatures to eat.

LITTLE MEAT-EATERS

Small killer dinosaurs use many different deadly hunting techniques.

▼ *Sinornithosaurus* may have grooved fangs, similar to a snake's.

▼ *Avimimus* is fast-moving and has a large brain for the size of its body, which suggests that it is capable of planning speedy surprise attacks.

▼ *Syntarsus* attacks in packs. By hunting in groups, it can bring down larger prey.

FLESH-EATING BULL

You find yourself face-to-face with a huge dinosaur—the horned *Carnotaurus*. It sniffs the air and then, as if it's caught a whiff of its prey or a competitor, it roars. Twisting its head, it glares at you. Perhaps your clothes hide the smell of your flesh because it pounds past, tracking the scent of something else. You follow from a safe distance in the ATV.

Carnotaurus' small horns are useful in a head-butting battle with a competing theropod or a fight with a rival over a mate.

It has sharp meat-tearing teeth but unusually weak jaws for a creature that needs to bite through skin and bone.

Carnotaurus is a meat-eater with an unusually weak jaw.

Meaning of name: Meat-eating bull
Height: 9 ft, 10 in (3 m)
Length: 25 ft (7.5 m)
Family: Abelisauridae
Period: Late Cretaceous
Weight: 1.1 tons (1,000 kg)
Found in: Argentina
Diet: Meat

The skin is a mass of pebble-like scales, becoming larger toward the spine. Skin impressions of nearly the entire body have given scientists an unusually clear idea of its bumpy skin.

TRACKING WITH THE SENSES

◀ The skull of the *Carnotaurus* shows it probably has an acute sense of smell—useful for tracking down its next live meal.

▶ Killer dinosaurs like *Carnotaurus* and *Tyrannosaurus* have simple ears—holes through which sound vibrations pass down nerve canals to the brain.

These stumpy arms are the shortest of any meat-eater.

▼ *Carnotaurus*, like other theropod dinosaurs, has forward-facing eyes. These give it binocular vision, which helps it to judge the distance of its prey.

HEAVYWEIGHTS

As you round an outcrop you come upon the *Carnotaurus'* prey: a spiky stegosaur. But another carnivore—an *Allosaurus*—is already on the scene. The *Allosaurus* tears at the plant-eater's vulnerable underbelly with its bladelike teeth. The stegosaur lashes out with its tail, but soon stumbles to the ground with exhaustion. You watch as the carnivores fight over its body.

A hungry *Allosaurus* won't be put off by the protective spikes of a stegosaur. However, it would prefer a sick or dead dinosaur that can't put up a fight.

Expandable cheeks mean that *Allosaurus* can bite off big chunks of meat to swallow whole.

Sharp serrated teeth, some twice the length of your finger, can cut through skin and flesh like a saw.

Allosaurus was at the top of the food chain in Jurassic times, and was the biggest carnivore on the planet for 10 million years.

Meaning of name: Different lizard
Height: 16 ft, 6 in (5 m)
Length: 40 ft (12 m)
Family: Allosauridae
Period: Late Jurassic
Weight: 1.5 tons (1,400 kg)
Found in: North America, Australia, Tanzania
Diet: Meat

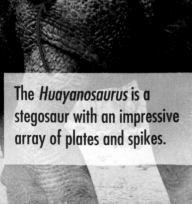

The *Huayanosaurus* is a stegosaur with an impressive array of plates and spikes.

SLOW COACHES
How fast can these big, heavy killers move?

► *Allosaurus* carries its huge weight on two feet. Fossils show that it often falls when running fast, so sprinting is probably used as a last option.

▼ Stegosaurs move at about 4.3 mph (7 km/h), while a short-armed theropod like the *Allosaurus* manages at least 20 mph (32 km/h).

► A giant sauropod like an *Apatosaurus* moves only as fast as a person walking. So to catch an *Apatosaurus*, the *Allosaurus* won't have to rush.

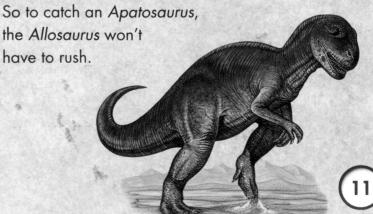

NIGHT HUNTERS

As night falls you set up infrared lights and wait silently to see what you can catch on film. Suddenly there's a roar, and sounds of a scuffle. A pack of *Troodon* surround a *Triceratops*! The *Troodon* pounce with their tearing, sickle-shaped claws, and serrated teeth—but the *Triceratops* puts up a tough fight. Soon the pack gives up, leaving to find easier game.

The plant-eating *Triceratops* relies on its sharp, 3 ft- (1 m-) long horns to scare off the attackers.

Troodon is seen as the brightest dinosaur, with the biggest brain in proportion to its body weight.

Troodon is an agile hunter with sharp claws on its hands and its feet.

Meaning of name: Wounding tooth
Height: 3 ft, 4 in (1 m)
Length: 6 ft, 6 in (2 m)
Family: Troodontidae
Period: Late Cretaceous
Weight: 100 lb (45 kg)
Found in: USA
Diet: Meat

Large, forward-facing eyes mean *Troodon* can judge distances easily. It seems to have good nocturnal vision.

SEEING IN THE DARK

▶ Big eyes suggest good nocturnal vision. The 1.5 ft- (0.5 m-) high *Dromaeosaurus* has huge eyes for the size of its body.

▼ Scientists measure rings of bone in the fossils of dinosaur eyes to estimate how well they could see in the dark. *Velociraptors* were probably among the dinosaurs that hunted at night.

▲ Eye fossil evidence suggests herbivores, such as *Diplodocus*, might have grazed at night too. To keep their vast bodies alive, long grazing hours may have been necessary.

TERRIFYING TYRANT

Your early morning alarm is a blood-curdling roar. You grab your camera, start up the ATV, and race toward the sound. It's the biggest dino movie star of them all: *Tyrannosaurus rex*. The monster's strong jaws pick up and shake its victim, an *Iguanodon*. The "tyrant lizard" uses its fanglike teeth to rip through the skin.

Tyrannosaurus teeth can crush bone. They can be up to 6 in (15 cm) long.

Stretch your arms wide and the length from fingertip to fingertip is about the length of the *Tyrannosaurus* jaw— 4.6 ft (1.4 m).

> *Tyrannosaurus rex* is the best known of all the dinosaurs.

Meaning of name: Tyrant lizard king
Height: 19 ft, 7 in (6 m)
Length: 46 ft (14 m)
Family: Tyrannosaur
Period: Late Cretaceous
Weight: 7.7 tons (7,000 kg)
Found in: North America
Diet: Meat

Tyrannosaurus' arms are too short to reach their mouths. However, they can be used for clutching prey or for steadying themselves as they stand up.

KILLERS' TEETH

▶ *Giganotosaurus*' teeth are smaller and narrower than the *Tyrannosaurus*' bone-crushers. However, they are better for slicing into the flesh of its prey.

▶ *Acrocanthosaurus* has 68 long, knifelike teeth. Like many theropods' teeth, they are curved and serrated. They are constantly shed and replaced by new teeth that grow in rows.

▶ *Dilophosaurus* has the teeth of a scavenger rather than a killer. The weak jaw and sharp teeth are better for plucking meat from a corpse and lack the strength to stab or grab a living dinosaur.

BATTLE TAILS

Another monster lumbers into view—an *Ankylosaurus*. The *T. rex* seems confused by the sudden appearance of this new opponent. As the predator hesitates, the *Ankylosaurus* swings its muscular tail toward its head. You duck as it whizzes past!

A two-legged predator like *T. rex* is especially vulnerable to *Ankylosaurus'* deadly club.

Ankylosaurus' back and sides are covered with thick armor. The *T. rex* aims to toss it onto its back.

WEAPON TAILS: CLUBS, WHIPS, AND SPIKES

Ankylosaurus is one of the most heavily armored dinosaurs ever found.

Meaning of name: Stiff lizard
Height: 4 ft (1.2 m)
Length: 23 ft (7 m)
Family: Ankylosauridae
Period: Late Cretaceous
Weight: 4.4 tons (4,000 kg)
Found in: Canada, USA
Diet: Plants

The knob at the end of the *Ankylosaurus'* tail is made up of bony plates fused together.

The "handle" of the club is made up of tendons that have partly turned to bone (ossified).

▶ **Tail clubs** Members of the ankylosaurid family, such as *Ankylosaurus*, are the best-known users of tail clubs. However, they are also used by dinosaurs such as the long-necked *Shunosaurus*.

◀ **Whip tails** *Brachiosaurus* flick out their long tails in a whiplike motion, knocking down predators. This gives them the opportunity to trample on their enemies while they are off-balance.

▶ **Tail spikes** Some plant-eaters, such as *Stegosaurus*, have tails ending with spikes. When threatened, a *Stegosaurus* will plant its back legs squarely, and use its front legs to swing its whole body, giving extra momentum to its tail.

FEET FIGHTERS

The epic battle ends in stalemate, and the *Tyrannosaurus* and *Ankylosaurus* leave, blood pouring from cuts and bites. As you walk back to the ATV, a group of fast-moving predators bursts through the bushes. These sleek raptors—called *Deinonychus*—are about your height, and they move fast. You only just make it to your ATV in one piece!

To bring down a smaller target, a raptor stabs a sickle claw into its victim, then drags it in a backward or downward motion across its flesh.

Deinonychus' sickle claws are so large they have to be raised when the dinosaur runs.

Deinonychus is far from the biggest dinosaur on the planet, but its intelligence, agility, and group hunting tactics made it one of the most fearsome.

Meaning of name: Terrible claw
Height: 5 ft (1.5 m)
Length: 10 ft (3 m)
Family: Dromaeosauridae
Period: Late Cretaceous
Weight: 180 lb (80 kg)
Found in: USA
Diet: Meat

CRUEL CLAWS

▼ The second toe on the *Deinonychus'* hind foot is unusually large—about 5 in (12 cm) long—and shaped like a sickle.

▼ *Velociraptor* is the most famous raptor. However, it is often misrepresented as being as tall as *Deinonychus*; in fact it is only about 3 ft (1 m) tall.

When a pack of *Deinonychus* jumps on a large victim, they use their hook claws like crampons. As they climb upward, they tear at vulnerable spots with their sharp teeth.

◄ *Troodon* is notable not just for its sickle claws, but also for its teeth, which have serrated sides like a saw.

SCAVENGING SWARM

Time to play it safe for a while. You drive the ATV up a sandy slope, and build a blind from branches. After a while, a swarm of *Coelophysis* rushes down the slope. Their tails sweep side-to-side like rudders. You follow, and see that they have discovered a carcass. Your camera records how they share their prey; some act as lookouts, while others take turns to eat.

These slim hunters with long tails and long necks are built to run fast. Like birds, they have hollow bones to keep them lightweight.

Coelophysis are not only hunters but probably scavengers too. Fossil contents of a *Coelophysis* stomach suggest that they could even be cannibals.

Coelophysis are known to gather together in packs. They may do this during the breeding season, and also to protect each other while feeding.

Coelophysis is a small carnivore. A flash flood in Mexico revealed the remains of lots of *Coelophysis* that died together.

Meaning of name: Hollow form
Height: 4 ft, 4 in (1.3 m)
Length: 10 ft (3 m)
Family: Coelophysoidea
Period: Late Triassic
Weight: 66 lb (30 kg)
Found in: USA
Diet: Meat

STRENGTH IN NUMBERS?

▼ Sauropod tracks show that the vulnerable young travel with older sauropods of the same species for safety.

▼ Gazelle-like in speed and size, *Hypsilophodon* find greater safety in numbers, as they can keep a better lookout for approaching hunters.

▼ Around 3,500 fossil bones (including 14 skulls) of *Pachyrhinosaurus* have been found in one area of Alberta. They migrate in herds seasonally, in search of food.

A clunk... a huge weight... and suddenly, you're knocked to the dusty ground. The roaring *Dilophosaurus* seem to be in a panic, and race past at about 25 mph (40 km/h). Fortunately, they don't notice you. What are they running from?

Dilophosaurus' dew claw is an unusual feature. It is similar to the dew claw found on the back of each leg on pet dogs and cats.

Weak jaws mean a weak bite, so this killer probably relies on its sharp claws to bring down its prey.

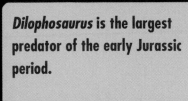

Dilophosaurus is the largest predator of the early Jurassic period.

Meaning of name: Two-ridged lizard
Height: 5 ft (1.5 m)
Length: 20 ft (6 m)
Family: Coelophysoidea
Period: Early Jurassic
Weight: 1,000 lb (450 kg)
Found in: USA
Diet: Meat

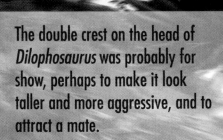

The double crest on the head of *Dilophosaurus* was probably for show, perhaps to make it look taller and more aggressive, and to attract a mate.

HOW MUCH DO WE KNOW?

What do we really know about the appearance of creatures like *Dilophosaurus*?

▶ The crests have never been found attached to the skull, but their position on top of the head is accepted by most scientists as likely to be correct.

▶ Some models of *Dilophosaurus* are covered with hair. Some evidence of hairlike and feather coverings have been found for some prehistoric creatures, such as the birdlike *Archaeopteryx*.

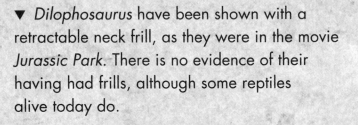

▼ *Dilophosaurus* have been shown with a retractable neck frill, as they were in the movie *Jurassic Park*. There is no evidence of their having had frills, although some reptiles alive today do.

AMBUSH!

You run up over the bank to see the creature the *Dilophosaurus* were terrified of. An *Albertosaurus*—a smaller relative of *Tyrannosaurus rex*—is lumbering along a lakeside. Just as you raise the camera, there's a roar and a splash. A *Deinosuchus* lunges up from the water and grabs its neck. The horror of it makes your head spin.

Another name for *Deinosuchus* is *Phobosuchus*, which means "horror crocodile." With a deadly gigantic 6.5 ft- (2 m-) long head, and an estimated body length of 33 ft (10 m), it's no wonder!

Albertosaurus was probably able to run at 25 mph (40 km/h) in spite of its size. Like *T. rex*, its teeth were not adapted to chewing, so it swallowed meat in large chunks.

Albertosaurus is a powerful killer and was one of the most common predators in Cretaceous North America.

Meaning of name: Alberta lizard
Height: 11 ft (3.4 m)
Length: 30 ft (9 m)
Family: Tyrannosauridae
Period: Late Cretaceous
Weight: 2.8 tons (2,500 kg)
Found in: North America
Diet: Meat

The *Deinosuchus* is a terrifying crocodile that hides in muddy waters, ambushing dinosaurs and snapping up turtles.

KILLING THE KILLERS

In Cretaceous times, hungry creatures lurked in wetland areas, waiting for passing dinosaurs.

▶ The 100 curved, bone-crunching teeth of the *Deinosuchus* can grasp the throat of a meat-eating dinosaur as it lowers its head to drink.

◀ Cretaceous crocodiles have eyes that can look up out of the water for prey, while their bodies are hidden under the water.

▼ The largest ever crocodile, *Sarcosuchus*, lives in Cretaceous times. Its conical teeth are perfectly shaped for grabbing small dinosaurs and holding them underwater until they drown, ready to be eaten.

ENDGAME

As you set off back to your ATV, the sky suddenly fills with fire. What's happening? A stampede of terrified dinosaurs thunders toward you... and everything goes black. When you come to, you find yourself on a boat heading home, clutching your camera. Perhaps you passed out and the fire-filled sky was all a dream. Or perhaps you just witnessed a new extinction of the dinosaurs.

WHAT KILLED THE DINOSAURS?

After ruling the Earth for 150 million years, the dinosaurs all suddenly died 65 million years ago. There are many theories as to what happened.

◄ A vast asteroid or comet may have collided with the Earth, causing a massive explosion, dust clouds, and shock waves. All around the world, plants and animals would have died.

► Scientists have discovered a vast crater in Mexico that probably formed when an asteroid or comet hit the Earth 65 million years ago. Its 112-mile (180-km) width suggests a catastrophic impact.

▼ In India there were huge volcanic eruptions at the time the dinosaurs died. Vast clouds of ash and dust may have screened out the sun. Plants would have died, then the plant-eaters, and finally the meat-eaters.

KILLER SAFARI REPORT

When you get home, you tell everyone about your safari experience. Crowds gather to hear of your terrifying encounters with killer dinosaurs. When you screen your film, gasps of disbelief fill the auditoriums. The images that get the biggest screams are those of the infamous *Tyrannosaurus rex*!

As you discovered, killers come in all sizes. The small swarming dinosaurs were as deadly as the huge, stumbling monsters. A swipe from the sickle-shaped claw of a 3.3 ft (1 m) *Troodon* could kill you as quickly as a bite from a 16.5 ft (5 m) *Allosaurus*.

- *T. rex*—19 ft, 7 in (6 m)
- *Allosaurus*—16 ft, 5 in (5 m)
- *Albertosaurus*—11 ft (3.4 m)
- *Carnotaurus*—9 ft, 10 in (3 m)
- Human—6 ft (1.8 m)
- *Deinonychus*—5 ft (1.5 m)
- *Dilophosaurus*—5 ft (1.5 m)
- *Troodon*—3 ft, 3 in (1 m)
- *Compsognathus*—2 ft, 4 in (0.7 m)

While on your safari, you saw creatures from many different parts of the prehistoric past. This chart shows the different periods in which they lived. MYA stands for million years ago.

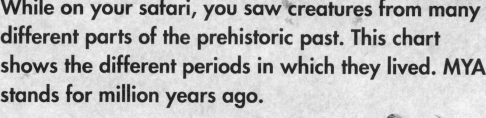

Troodon

Compsognathus

Carnotaurus

Tyrannosaurus rex

Ankylosaurus

Deinonychus

Albertosaurus

Dilophosaurus

Allosaurus

Coelophysis

TODAY	
QUATERNARY	1.5 mya
TERTIARY	65 mya
CRETACEOUS	150 mya
JURASSIC	205 mya
TRIASSIC	250 mya
PERMIAN	290 mya
CARBONIFEROUS	355 mya
DEVONIAN	410 mya
SILURIAN	440 mya
ORDOVICIAN	510 mya
CAMBRIAN	570 mya
PRECAMBRIAN	4,600 mya

GLOSSARY

asteroid A rocky object that orbits the Sun. Asteroids can crash into other planets, such as Earth.

ATV (all terrain vehicle) A three- or four-wheel bike with an engine, soft wheels, and handlebars for off-road travel (also called a quad or quad bike).

binocular vision The way in which the world is seen through two forward-facing eyes, which helps an animal judge distance.

blind A shelter used to hide in while watching wildlife, such as birds.

Brachiosaurus A giant four-legged plant-eater from the Jurassic age.

breeding season Months in the year when animals gather in order to create offspring.

cannibals Animals that eat the flesh of their own kind.

comet An object of ice and dust that travels in space and forms a tail of gas and dust as it passes close to the Sun.

conical Describing a round, pointed shape such as an ice-cream cone.

crampons Spikes that are attached to the bottom of climbers' shoes to grip rock, snow, or ice.

Cretaceous A prehistoric period in which mammals and giant dinosaurs such as *Tyrannosaurus rex* lived, which ended with

the mass extinction of the dinosaurs 65 million years ago.

dew claw A claw that does not reach the ground but is positioned higher than the foot, at the back of the leg.

duckbills Dinosaurs with jaws that are shaped like a duck's bill (beak); also called hadrosaurids.

fangs Long, sharp teeth, which are often used for biting and tearing flesh.

fossils Prehistoric remains such as bones, or traces such as footprints, that have become preserved in rock.

horns Pointed bones that stick out from a creature's head, which can be used for attack or defense.

lizard A four-legged reptile with scaly skin and a long tail, such as a chameleon.

mate One of two animals (a male or a female) that have come together to have offspring (babies).

nocturnal vision The ability to see in the dark.

scavenger A creature that feeds on rubbish or dead material, such as the flesh of dead dinosaurs.

serrated With a jagged edge, like the edge of a saw.

shock waves A violent change in air pressure that travels outward from an explosion, causing damage and destruction.

Shunosaurus A four-legged plant-eating dinosaur from the Jurassic age, with a long tail that ends in a spiked club.

sickle A curved shape like the sickle tool, which was used on farms for cutting crops.

skin impressions The shapes made by the surface of the skin: for example the shapes of scales or feathers on a dinosaur, which are preserved as fossils.

stegosaur Four-legged plant-eating dinosaurs, such as *Stegosaurus*, which have two rows of bony plates down their back, a short neck, and small head.

tendons Tough, ropelike tissue in bodies, such as the tissue that attaches muscles to bones.

therapod Two-footed, mainly meat-eating, dinosaurs such as *Tyrannosaurus* and *Giganotosaurus*.

FURTHER READING

Dinosaur Encyclopedia by Caroline Bingham (Dorling Kindersley, 2009)

Dinosaur Experience by John Malam (Dorling Kindersley, 2006)

Dinosaurus: The Complete Guide to Dinosaurs by Steve Parker (Firefly, 2009)

Tyrannosaurus Rex Vs Velociraptor: Power Against Speed (Dinosaur Wars) by Michael O'Hearn (Raintree, 2011)

The Mystery of the Death of the Dinosaurs (Can Science Solve?) by Chris Oxlade (Heinemann Library, 2008)

Predators (Dinosaur Files) by John Malam (Dorling Kindersley, 2009)

WEB SITES

www.kidsdinos.com/ Dinosaurs for Kids—fun facts, games and a dinosaur database

www.nhm.ac.uk/kids-only/dinosaurs/index.html London's Natural History Museum—includes a dinosaur directory and quiz

www.amnh.org/exhibitions/fightingdinos/—information about the American Museum of Natural History's "Fighting Dinosaurs"

http://dsc.discovery.com Discovery Dinosaur Central—search the DinoViewer for size comparisons and how dinosaurs moved

http://ngm.nationalgeographic.com National Geographic—search for the Bizarre Dinosaur section for a closer look at strange dinosaurs

http://www.enchantedlearning.com/subjects/dinosaurs/ Zoom Dinosaurs—basic to advanced information on dinosaurs and prehistory

INDEX